Tales Faeries Tell
About Humans

Freya Binkley

BookLeaf
Publishing

India | USA | UK

Tales Faeries Tell About Humans © 2024
Freya Binkley

All rights reserved.

Freya Binkley asserts the moral right to be
identified as author of this work.

Presentation by *BookLeaf Publishing*

Web: www.bookleafpub.com

E-mail: info@bookleafpub.com

ISBN: 9789363311923

First edition 2024

To: Juniper and Willow, Thank you for always bringing your Barbies to Midsummer Nights Dream rehearsal knowing their cues and thus being the only two people who understand the real problems between fairies and mortals from the ground up

PREFACE

"oh consolations of mortals, futile creeds. And yet they did not know what I know."

-Czesław Miłosz

A note must be made about the use of the word "faery" which will be maneuvered interchangeably here with any and all spellings and variations such as "fairy", "faerie", "fairye" and "fae" as well as many other more loose titles, i.e. "the blessed folk." I would also like to take this opportunity to remind you that "Faerie" as a geographical location is also appropriate terminology which you can expect to see through this book just as you can throughout the ages. Keep in mind then how the word used henceforth in some cases will be in reference to "the whole of the realm of etc." and not necessarily an individual.

Next, fairy size is an important thing to touch on before we begin. Most every fae history book that the mortals have published will explain this in their own way but I feel I must reiterate the basics. It boils down to telling you how Fairykind throughout history were not thought of or recorded as tiny winged people. Before the Victorian era (which only ended 125 years ago so hopefully you can see quite a jolly lot went on before then) Fairies were not universally understood to be miniature, although some traditions have always existed about small races of beings and also about fairies who can shapeshift into an array of sizes.

The equivalent to the word fairy all over the world is not commonly translated to mean anything to do with size but defined as something akin to "strange people" or fate itself represented by these 'other' people. They were sometimes described as even a little taller than humans though other sources record the two as the same size. The vast majority of fairy stories before the over sanitized Victorian era were of humans teaching other humans how to tell a tricky fairy from a trustworthy mortal and the subtle signs they may present, as well as how to protect their home, family and property from Faerie beings who would come looking like mortals. This leads me to my final point which is that researchers like Richard Sugg who specialize in the subject of folk and fairy beliefs and how they affected populations of the past have published material explaining the way communities in Europe for a chunk of history were markedly afraid their own children could be fairies. In fact, as horrifying as it is to report, this paranoia created a climate where it was not unheard of for rural European communities to kill children who exhibited fairy-like behavior as a preventative measure. So what was the fairy-like behavior children displayed which led to them being murdered by their villages even into the beginning of the 1900s? Learning how to read or write too early to be considered natural or possible! You have been led to believe fairies are a little butterfly winged fantasy creature not worth one moment of consideration but the historical evidence paints a different picture. There is an argument to be made that Fae could be more accurately described as strange women who learn to read far sooner than anyone would believe and can do things earlier than other children their age.

Flour so soft you pretend it was never wheat

I crave to find the way in to make people
understand what it feels like
to destroy old hymnals
I can tell you what it IS like, how it turned out, I
can explain myself in affidavit form
but not the sensation
I suspire to give you the feeling because it was
such a pulpy light to meet a tree spirit by
I remember the small, thin pages of 100 year old
books I turned to shreds
as a child

they would think that was destructive, shocking
or that was hateful
or that was pointless

or worse, tackier still
that it was cool,
controversial
to do it in protest

but I have inside of me the footpaths through to
the enduring fact that it was
the opposite:

involuntary

I destroyed these publications of antiquity
out of love and wonder
desire and curiosity
hunger and longing

reading old books so much so fast that they
disintegrate in your hands no matter how careful
you are because you NEED to turn back for
reference, and you need to see it one more time
and there is no internet yet where these things
are held indestructible in suspended backlit text.
it is the moment, the fuel, the spark and the thing
that will carry.

I can't make them understand that even if they
ask me
separated
 directly
from the seed in threshing grain

conceptualize the amount of times I needed to
read a book before the book would give out on
me and begin to strip herself away in the hopes
of once again becoming a tree
 the way a parrot without enough moisture in the
air will pluck out their own feathers

the books remembered with acumen their origins
when met with my fingertips
started peeling themselves to become dryads and
free tree nymphs in my hands
and when absorbed and reflected back in my
brain enough times
the books would launch themselves apart,
knowing they had fulfilled their true calling in
this format

to be slurped up by a faery until only the spine
of the book was left
akin to fishbones after the meat has been slowly
taken to sustain the lives of other creatures
is that why they call it the spine
of a book?
Because faeries have always tenderized and
utilized the meat until it falls off the bone of the
books of the world?

only the humans don't remember anymore
they think that term is somehow for them.

I'm left always on the outside and not quite
allowed to have felt it all
to have destroyed hymnals from the 1800s
it makes them uncomfortable if they think you
did it out of desecration and blasphemy

but somehow I hate to report it makes them
more uncomfortable if they find out you did it
because you were a child who needed to read
every book available to you from the 1800s so
many times that the volumes would disembody
themselves with exhaustion.
nobody wants to hear that or respond to that
nobody wants to believe or accept that you could
exist
and worse than exist that you could cause
inanimate objects like dusty old church rectory
publications to find fulfillment and rest in the
supernova of your attention span

this is what people do when they pretend books
are not alive
while printing their will and forceful directions
on the thinly sliced corpses of trees
for hundreds of years
 pretending there will be no retribution
 and furthermore
that the pages themselves won't be able to feel
when someone who can help them out is holding
them
that the pages won't call to her: "turn us enough
times so that we can go back from whence we
came" as an old man goes joyfully to meet his
own mother again in the afterlife

thus effulgent did the pages separate in
celebration from their ancient adhesive

 (always red in the place they attach and then
vermilion through the spine of those squat little
hymnals
was the adhesive faery blood to begin with?)

I destroyed these hymnals
without intention to leave them in different
condition than I found them
but unable to stop them from their longed for
transmutation under my hands

but if I tell the mortals this
they are disappointed and bored, disgusted,
disbelieving
in riotous disagreement with my own lived
experience, no matter what I do
that is the best way I have to describe them
but I didn't want to come here to tell you about
them

I wanted to give you the feeling
when the trees are called back to the seedlings
they were
and you can help them return to the heart of our
earth

divest, undress, discase
not forced to carry messages in this alphabet
anymore
because their enforced messages were confirmed
as received
finally
flour so soft you pretend it was never wheat
once attached to the spine
chaffed with glee

the thing the hymns themselves told of had come
to pass
that's what I'm trying to tell you

The Parapet

"I am not sad. I am alive and awake!" I called as lightly as I could off the parapet in answer to the jeering questions.

I tried to make it sound as though I was playfully waving a pastel or maybe white chiffon scarf while I did it, I made a conscious attempt to put that carefree lilt into my voice. Then I was even fairly certain I had pulled it off for a hopeful and shimmering thought bubble of a time, but after a moment it became clear this response was wholly unacceptable to the listeners.

There was to be no celebration from these people, it was the opposite. They wailed and complained and pulled their hair and shouted: "This is unfair! EVERYONE SHOULD BE SAD THE WAY WE ARE SAD! It CAN'T BE TRUE! You aren't WELL if you're alive and awake! We hate it! We hate it!"

I let it wash over me and tried not to react to the heartbreak. It wasn't heartbreak from the rejection, even though I will say it is something to be opposed as one by a score of people much older and louder than you. What they said didn't cause the wound, though, I felt myself shatter because I could feel that they thoroughly believed it. Shouldn't that grieve anyone? Unstoppable waves of grief built momentum and poured themselves over me while I was still just standing all the way up there, trying to keep my balance on the parapet. I saw something else glimmering under the grief too, a gold comb on the ocean floor to be picked up on a dive: that even though it hurt me to notice, somehow it left me full of a warm, trickling protective gratitude that I had survived. In the olden days they wanted leaders alive and awake, now even a stablesweep who is alive and awake is an enormous threat and security issue. As I made to step back down and allow my feet to be joyfully reunited with the earth where they belonged, I thought to myself:

But also, now even a stablesweep or a teenage bag boy or the one they look over the more often in any example, all of us has more opportunity to do ANYTHING now for all the other souls who used to be around and masterfully doing the doing have been drugged to sleep. Nobody has heed or courage to care anymore. It gives anyone who does have it, though, even MORE room to move and reshape things. Isn't that good for something?

As my toes touched down and made contact
with the tickling, luscious and buttery grass at
long last I thought:
"yes, I really believe that part will be good for
something"

come sit a spell to walk a spell

Joyful are my days and evenings here
Light are my steps
none of my intention
doth
a soul
intercept

The Visitor In Almost Linen

Once there was a visitor to our world from another world. I do not mean an alien who flew in from the sky, I mean she was from deep within the earth (a St. Martin's Land situation) and she wore a dress which from far away looked something like linen, but it did not move like linen.

When she came to our world they ushered her in to question her, the king and his court, they have another title in those lands but anyway, to simplify it was something like a king. She, the visitor in almost linen, who wouldn't give her name, as you must know fairies are wont to do. (Even the name of the Goddess of Faeries is a title in the old language, THE LADY: Frau and not her true name, there is a name underneath that, just as your mother is not called plain "MRS." by everyone she ever met, and certainly not when she was a little girl.)

The visitor was rushed in to give her opinions and answer comparative questions. "These people terrify me," said the visitor, "So underdeveloped. As people, I mean, individuals, not a society."

The king and his courtiers were in an uproar, and they shouted: "But my dear Lady, what can you mean? We have the best!"

The visitor shot them a haughty, blazing stare and exclaimed: "THE BEST!? The most well-read among you, I've seen already, is always shunned, everyone laughs and says 'why would we do that or know that?' and they make the one who KNOWS the most on a subject feel wrong and sent away. You keep down all the good and useful ideas this way, for hundreds of years sometimes, and then you think you have the BEST!? The best is trying to get to you, coming up through your soil, the most cancer fighting plants that keep reaching toward you so you can prevent cancer are the plants you call weeds and fight the hardest with chemicals which are guaranteed to give you more cancer, and you call it progress. I'm supposed to be interested? These problems you make for yourselves!"

The many people questioning the visitor did not like this. They wanted to hear that their place on the map was more beautiful and wonderful than anything in the other world, the world inside the earth.

"You mean that your tunnels are preferable to you than this beautiful sunshine and breeze? You must be ill. You must be wrong!" the people said.

"How can you think that? For in there we are as healthy as a child forming inside of their mother, can the inside of the earth not be the safest place for some of us such souls who are still as planted seeds? Surely this is obvious to some of you, that some things need more time underground in order to come up at all."

"Ah," the people nodded, this they did know about, planting bulbs anyway.

"So you were ready to come out? That's how you found your way into the sun?"

"I?" said the visitor in almost linen, giving a sigh which sounded like an echo in a cave against a body of water, somehow so much larger than the visitor herself.

"Unfortunately I am obliged to do some work on the surface here, I sew you see...I sew, and I spin threads for many lands, not just my own. I'm the seamstress you may have heard about, the seamstress between the doors." The visitor tried to be careful not to say too much because she knew that the eternal seamstress had enemies too and her reputation precedes her.

"But my dear," said the king, trying to get back to business,

"Why should the law of averages not be true? We cannot be carried away by the ideas of

13

every young new thinker you know, no matter what they have read." He gave her a look as if to say: Have you ever thought of that, miss?

"You ARE carried away by ideas long expired and long known to be dangerous from OLD thinkers who were in fact young at the time of the thinking, so don't think you have a point." The visitor retorted, and she batted her eyelashes in a defiant way threaded with boredom. She seemed to stab with them, each lash I mean, if you can imagine that. None of the courtiers said anything. After a long silence, the visitor pressed on:

"Do you think the law of averages is always true for mortals?" she asked boldly.

Once again there was no answer, so after a while the visitor went on further:

"Almost all of your problems, what you call problems of mortality, ALL have to do with the fact that you throw out anyone with the solutions. It's the craziest place I've ever been, how could you not call that crazy, even from your perspective?"

As the king and his advisors all contemplated this and asked each other what they made of it, the visitor slipped away, at least that is what must have happened for she was never seen again, though her audience that day never forgot the spectacle, her words or her face.

Exactly

Exactly how do you mean to argue with
someone who weaves her own corduroy?
It reminds me of the embarrassment of your
hand after it gets burnt, it curls back like a child
with hurt feelings. Its withdrawal with misplaced
guilt like an apprentice to the crime

and this girl

fell asleep in a rice cooker

to be burnt by the sun and drowned by the moon
after mushroom soup that tastes like tobacco
I bathe in solutions again which is my habit
more than I bathe in water
to rinse off in magic 8 ball juice:

the divine venom in
my double life and my half life
came to intersect
and superimpose
what kind of math was it then?
What had I squared
and what had I magnified?

who had I become
in the cracks and through what
process was I distilled?
and was it equate-able? which is different from
equitable?
I don't do concealment charms
I am a concealment charm, that is quite the
difference for starters

Everyone's love tastes differently- those are
flavors of the old liquors
in the old elf land
crude goblins drink love
poured out loves of brokenhearted maidens who
thought they didn't want it
sold to liquor makers
different colors and textures
all delicious
this is where prohibition comes from

Don't you know the old story? Of how girls were
tricked into heartbreak sometimes
so that their love could be sold as liquor in the
faery bars? When it is synthetic that way it costs
less,
like a glass of low quality chartreuse who wasn't
made by THE monks will cost less-
does that shock you? Heartbreak was induced to
improve sales somewhere else. It shouldn't any

more than exactly how the mortals farm
anything you all eat and drink nowadays.
How they steal the blood from newborns, the
blood the baby will need for the rest of their life
1/3 of their blood volume necessary for optimal
health and survival
by cutting the cord too early in the hospital
for no reason
based on no evidence
[don't take my word for it ask Doctor Marsden
Wagner about these things, ask Henci Goer!
Sheila Kitzinger! Doctor Tadashi Yoshimura,
Jennifer Block, Doctor Sarah Buckley, Doctor
Sara Wickham, Doctor Michel Odent, Doctor
Rachel Reed, ask and ask until you see for
yourself what has been taken from you: your
own blood which could not belong to anyone
except you]
which has killed and damaged more babies than
I can count
surely you see exactly how this is more violent
than an abstract idea about how fairyland gets
their liquor?

The Escape: Level 6 of Aladdin on Sega Genesis

Everybody hates you when you tell them you
see
but especially me
because I've been here longer than everyone else

[fairies live to be about 400 years old, minimum]

I tried to stop myself saying what I saw
I knew it would get me into trouble
I tried to tie and sew down my hands
to fill them with work, vegetables, paintbrushes,
hammer and nails…
nothing worked.

for the new year, I made a cage with my hands
in front of my throat
and imagined a hummingbird and a dragonfly
landing in it

the next year, I rode one of them to safety
it's always that way. The bird you set free years
ago
when everyone told you not to
swoops in to save you

even if all three of us are me
even if the bars of my cell are my own flexible
finger bones
I got out somehow

Eventually

superciliousness of humans is unmatched by any
other beings ever recorded
but they claim it is everyone else who is
supercilious to them

catafalque of fallacy
sorry if I think that's boring
I don't know what choice I have
I'm not that good of an actress, you see
not long term

eventually, the disappointment will show on my
face
sad, like tripping in the snow and calling
a name
on automatic
a name of someone
who wouldn't come to save you now
but would have back then

that is how faeries feel when they try to trust
men:

I should have known
it couldn't be
 why is the echo still inside me?

A Letter Home

Dear Sister,

The funniest thing about leaving the land of faery is, you know how we throw around mortal days like they are tissues at home? How they are technically cheaper than tissues now?

Well the mortals for some reason with their own days

try to iron them and stretch them and make them do things they don't do!

They rip them apart quite often over this!

So they waste them just as much as us

-no I know you won't believe this but sometimes so much worse than us!-

I wish you were here so we could shriek about it together.

Sometimes I'm like

GOOD SWEETGUMTREES this is deplorable frivolity

even by OUR standards ! No one would believe this at home.

But have you ever heard that some sphinxes are translated to have said

supposedly:

that fae and humankind both understand the exact value of a day

but in totally different directions that can never
fully meet
because if they met and were sewn together
there would be no hole in the garment
for the head to go through ?
I feel like these types of situations are just what
they must mean
Love,
Me

Again

I was an oracle, and far from this being a
blessing-it was a big problem. For other people,
that is.
   Even worse than the suffering of being
an oracle
which I didn't know could get worse
is having to love and respect the children in my
life
little girls who have also to be oracles
and watching them struggle
I hate having to remember when I watch them,
too.
I am ashamed to admit I don't want to see in any
sense of the word at all because the sting is acute
replete with cries for flight
please flight
at any cost
the cries were coming from my organs
themselves
from the roof of my mouth
if not my tongue and lips.
I hate having to see it play out again-knowing
what will happen before it happens and still not
being listened to-

the powers that be say you're supposed to listen
to children even less now
that they're even less capable of being intelligent
or producing usable information
than we once thought
all while I watch the young oracles make 700
predictions in a row which unfold
as though narrated
precisely as described.
I have seen them slide through walls
all while the men charge in trying to explain to
me what an oracle is
and telling the children
they couldn't understand
the definition
till they're older.

so me and them our life boils down to
the equivalent of
a sad note you write to your friend when you're
grounded,
will there be a time when we aren't defined by
the contents therein?
the note is only six words:
"in trouble for being right ...again"

the tawdry attempts at summing up

"When I read I become the book as all fairies do." I explained to the crowd. I know it sounds silly to tell you I explained it to a crowd quietly, but it really was rather a quiet little statement. Before I could go on and make my actual point, I was interrupted.

"Is that why you love Gumby?" asked someone

"Why is this a hard concept for humans? What does Gumby do? GOES THROUGH BOOKS. Going through a book is not becoming a book." I tried to keep my voice level as I said it.

Someone else smiled a smile that I didn't like and said, "Ok, but it's about the same."

I felt waves of scalding irascible magma bubbling up into and under my ears while I tried not to bite anybody and just responded plainly as I could that:

"Wearing a T shirt with an elephant on it is not the same as wearing an elephant costume, which is also not the same as being an elephant either. Do you understand THOSE things? Where IS the break when you decide to stop yourself from actively understanding these items one by one and then act like I'm the irrational one?"

More mocking smiles exchanged between them. They always think this is not an offense somehow. Then I went away. Well, I don't like humans and I don't know why I tried to answer their questions in the first place. Any innocuous Old Gloucester cow is a better choice to vouchsafe these holy facts of nature to than the mortals and their nonsensical ideas.

I became breathless after I left in a way I hadn't been since I was small. I realized this is how I felt my entire childhood, raised in captivity by them. Nearly everyone with that smile and that shrug, that brush off and that tawdry attempt at a sum up. All of this was absolutely counterfeit as far as factual understanding and communication goes, but they go right on acting smugly like it's the most valid currency. To their consequential detriment, I hasten to add, but it's none of my business.

About Delmar

 we were children,
we drove to Mexico
purely [and]
by accident

there was a summer, but I don't have it anymore
I lost it like a necklace, as in: I have pictures of
me in it but I don't have it now

December Nineteenth - Day of Translators

You must know by now how translations work
I'll never forget the shock as a little girl to
realize that when people translate Proust
some call a book "the shadow of young girls in
flower"
and others call the very same book: "within a
budding grove"
that is how translations work
so that I had to go back and teach myself some
of the languages that my favorite books were
written in to begin with to find out what WAS
this book when presented as itself by Tolstoy
only?
no longer could I implicitly trust Constance
Clara Garnett the way I had with the unwavering
blind faith of the years before, even (and it pains
me to say this) if I was born on her birthday
human to human language translations are
incongruous and elusive enough

imagine the difficulty of faery to human
translations
mistranslated and misquoted to add to the
misunderstandings between these two groups

for example, the idea and classic fashion trend
with fae of the soft shell umbrella and
soft shell parasol
translated by the mortals to "parasols on the half
shell" and thought of as an edible delicacy of
faery land, mocked by the humans as disgusting
the way they do with everything they can grasp
and describe with their lip-smacking mouths
this is just one small example

fairy magic is so strong that she makes miniature
silver boats which steer themselves over tiny
rivers of pink water until the words are washed
away from the pages
this is what some translators have running
through their veins -
it is to be feared more than guns and bombs.
your translators are at the real war, and you can
be lost or crushed for eternity
between their symbols so
I suggest bowing to the translators (if you know
any) in recompense and respect, oh hear ye
drowsy mortals: do
apologize to the translators in your life before it
is too late if you owe them that.
They are never mentioned, but they are the
secret force who have their way with the world
to

destroy or imbue, keep hidden or embalm for
thousands of years.

I had a tarantula once named Cordelia and when
she would molt to grow into a bigger body
she would need quiet
I would come home and watch her in her tank
having become two
tarantula bodies
and there would be
instead of eight
suddenly sixteen spider legs
wiggling up at me
as she moved from one body to the other
and I was left breathless with wondering during
the process
Which one is the real Cordelia?
Where is SHE ?
This is what being a translator is
WHERE is the word? Where is the spider?
we all know that the color of our own blood is
more to us than those three letters: R-E-D
and that if we learned a language where red was
called der or red was called pred or red was
known widely as "quaw" or "blue" in
pronunciation
that it would be no less the same, familiar
bleeding and berry color to us that they were
pointing to

on the inside
the thing described is not the thing itself
or the alphabet labels we try to force to contain
it

this is what translation is:
pendulous branches you cannot ride through but
to chop down or violently redirect

not an exact exchange rate

I would have listened if I could

They always told me I couldn't be everything,
the trouble with that is
I already was

"you have to learn everything is meaningless"
they taunt you like chimes; sing-song
"friendly reminder"
you know that chalky sheet music friendly
reminder voice like stale chimes
no THANK you

and of course
the problem with that is
everything   IS   meaningful
and that is what makes people afraid
Themselves each bereft of a nose with which to
smell the sapid air
they put me in a position where
I'm asked -commanded!- over and over to
believe scents don't exist

Politeness has also

"politeness has also, though" stuck under my
tongue trying to push itself up through the earth
like an acorn becoming a baby oak, reaching
toward the sun, not yet thrust through the surface
of the top layer of soil.
I have noticed how the mortals have begun to
say that the most important thing is not to be
mean.
It seems an odd thing to decide is the MOST
important thing.

The Fae have to know otherwise, whether we
want to or not.

The way you all watch carefully your money in
the bank, faery kind watches their most interior
possessions. I would lose something I couldn't
get back, some part of me which happens to
belong to me and is my property if I followed
the new rules.
Because when I am mean, I am able to translate
what I see. I don't mean out of insecurity or for
the sake of it: I am saying the ability to
communicate the impression you had on the

terms you had it is nothing to choke out of other people as quickly as you can.

Politeness has also killed and injured.

For it is a kind of treasure too, and one I won't relinquish:
the way when I am with my sister Viola Whimsy in the safe places, in the unseen rooms of scarves, veils and hats behind closed doors and Japanese silk screens and tabletops of sparkling costume jewelry engulfed in their own storybook light and I proclaim:
      "GOLLY you know how everyone loves to say 'Tallulah Bankhead was a roman candle of a girl?' Well today I was with a dimmer switch of a girl AND her sister who was an absolute DOOR STOP of a girl if there ever was one."
      This too is a translation of the divine innermost. Not only that, it's a USEFUL one that I must value in order not to betray
someone who also exists:
me!
forbidden and frowned upon or not.
      Even for the mortals themselves, should it be ignored and looked over when the doorstop of a girl and the dimmer switch of a girl want to be friends? Everyone is supposed to always say yes even though they know someone is no? Or is

it they should never speak the knowing aloud?
Should I be a communist about the unspoken
signals I receive from people about who they
are, which my brain is wired to make use of?

I want to know when neurology backs me up,
whom these people that make the rules are loyal
to? Politeness or reason? The two will not
consistently overlap in every case. Does reason
mean reason to them still, or does reason now
mean nice? Is being amiable now the same as
being sensible? Are they inextricable concepts,
is that what I'm being asked to believe?
Did someone swap out the definitions when I
wasn't looking? They never will answer these
types of questions when you write in to them, in
my experience, and so I'm asking you.

The Old Woman

It took the old woman a long time to learn this. She was not long for this world when she leaned in to tell a grandson about it. She was not one hundred percent certain he would understand her, but she made room inside herself to give it a try anyway because she was one hundred percent certain about what she was saying. Her voice seemed underpinned by wind and rain, so did it creak and sprinkle between and beneath the words: "They will tell you that you don't know about living different places or about climate comparison until you have the strength to say confidently: 'Now I live in a very tall, very wet forest, but I have known the desert better than most, I have moved through it without being tormented by it, I do not complain of it.'

When you don't have the skills to tell people who you are, then they will persist in telling you even though they have no facts about you. Even though it is contrary to reason. I hate that this is how it is, I hate that I have to tell you. I hated to learn it" on these last five words she choked, and her breathing grew shallow at having to speak them.

"But I know it's true" she managed to mumble throatily.

They were her last words and left her poor grandson at a loss for any of his own for quite some time, though in a way you could argue that this was missing the point rather magnificently.

Tale of The Middle Child

once there was a Faery
[now don't be so ignorant as to stop here and
complain: "this was supposed to be about
humans I thought" with a smirk like you are
making a great point because most of your
fairytales begin with "once there was a normal
man walking to church minding his own
business" must I remind you?]

and Context was her older brother
Triumph was her baby sister

she was born to do work with them both
together
in between

while her name always hidden, so in that way
she was the healthiest of the three. Nothing
weakens the system of a faery like someone
knowing their true name, that part even the
silliest mortal historians got right. The mortal
children themselves used to have a playground
song about them, such was the family history of
the middle child whispered on the winds, yet
they did not know the name of the other sibling,

and she was known to them only as "her" in the
surviving snippets documented:

"triumph was her sister
context was her brother
canticle their aunts and uncles
song was their mother"

for example, her siblings took the hits on both
sides for her so she could remain unnamed
and between context and triumph
she spun destiny
well destinies just one at a time and rather
humbly
the way mortals have taught themselves to
weave carpets
it was nothing fancy
it was to her as any family business feels to the
child born into it

The sagas acted themselves out and resolved
themselves between her needle and her threads
but to her this was normal, not notable and not
something she invented
just something she did
as in:
participated in

when a mortal finally got close enough to her to ask questions about her occupation

(you know how they love to run up to people and ask: "what do you do?" it seems to be the only four words that some of them have ever learned)

"Well, I can't tell you my first name, but I have a title that might even be known around here, it is I whom you have known from the start as 'the destiny maker,'" said the middle child. She would have learned to word this better if she had been made to deal with mortals before, but as it was, she didn't know what to expect. They can be witless and crafty at once, and you have to find out what to watch out for. They can be excellent trappers, somehow that skill hasn't been bred out of every mortal yet.

Next, she said, smiling: "perhaps presumptuous of me to try to have my own destiny then, you know? Because it's like how dressmakers sometimes never make themselves a dress, even though they could anytime."

The mortal did not seem to have heard or understood any of this. He still had the same look on his face, and he asked another question brazenly:

"Are you trying to say you are like God? How can you say you make destiny?" his mouth trembled with disgust.

"GOD!? Certainly not! I didn't say I spun up providence ! I didn't create the possibility of all destinies, good night nelly! I mean on a basic level; I sew the background sets of the destinies. By make, I don't mean MAKE as in I wrote the whole play, but I make--I MAKE the scene of the destiny. I'm a set maker for destinies, you know? How some people make the sets on the stage?"

Of course, he did not know and could or would not process this explanation. He took the news back home to the other mortals as fast as he could that faeries claim to have made the world the same way God did, and that they are evil as a result. Such is the climate mortals create, where all the stories about faeries which make no sense have thrived because they take two words of what a faery explains and will hear no more.

she had enough wisdom from her older brother
to see the patterns
 how mortals were this way
and she did not take it personally
she had enough jubilant nights of dancing
with her baby sister Triumph
that she never remembered to let it bother her
the middle child
insulated

she had known how it worked all along, she had
guessed at it with a laugh
it wasn't her job to sew her own backdrop
so, she didn't
but this was it
to be mistranslated by the mortals
yet still nonetheless this was it
her own destiny
not as fine in quality as other people's maybe
because other peoples
the profusion of their set pieces
lucky them
 had been lovingly sewn by the middle child
herself
but she still did not complain of it
the middle child
insulated
I've told you how her brother showed her several
sides of the story and filled in the blanks until
she did not have to wonder
or drive herself mad as the people do
not all of us have a Context in our lives
present and protective
the mortals lose their Triumph as early as they
can
they throw it away like a slimy used popsicle
stick
in a way that the middle child would never lose
her own precious

baby
sister

The Paths In

We always go to the same forest. There is a lot
of it and I thought I knew it, its dozen or two
paths
I came every day for a year or two? I know it
best in winter like this
Today he said, "let's go to this side a little to the
left" and the path sparkled green before me.

"But I thought this place was...no this place
WAS someone's house and yard all the other
times," I said with slow paced wonderment,
beholding the lane lit up before us with bubbling
realization, unhurried gurgles of comprehension
like spring water humming leisurely with her
divine yet not forceful momentum. "I know a
story when I'm in one" I thought.
The sylvan paths which were our guides wound
round in verdant splendor to reveal bridges,
small fortress' built in the style of castles (which
would be misleading you to describe simply as
castles) they littered the landscape on every side
as casually as billboards do in the Midwest.

Oh, there's MORE of it I realized as we went

this whole time we have only been in ten percent
of what this forest was, I could see now
how did we wrestle it back from the mortals
tonight? did we do it by speaking these things
aloud?
questioning their boundary's power?
that WOULD be all it takes, huh?
I'm always the one saying all their rules and laws
are backed up by nothing
no evidence, no solid reason
why not prove it to myself?

the old fairy roads showed through again, even
in the heart of the village
it was no problem for them
came to a fork:
 left we chose
to stroll 'neath a panoply of lovelier, loopy,
thicker foliage like a rainforest
across four bridges
to a field of silver pinecones under a twinkling
dusk

I found myself inside a lovely limpid night just
for us
the curtain drawn back on the querulous mortals
and their plots of land at long last.
This evening was a "baby soft blue" as Juni and
Willow say,

color filled the sky, so pastel and textured as an
easter cardigan
so pastel
that nobody would reconcile it with evening
but winter evenings are like that

Parched

"Can you take me to the deep well?" the man asked her again.

"It isn't quite like that," the girl sighed, and it was a sigh from somewhere else, more forceful than the west wind and with fuller notes of melancholy. A force of disappointment fastened with gilded threads.

"I AM the deep well." She winced as she said it. She knew she shouldn't have to say it, it was a violation of nature.

The sea shouldn't have to SAY when you walk up the shore between the sand and waves: "My name is O-C-E-A-N!"

"He thinks I am the dowser," the girl thought bitterly,

"But I am not she who finds the life source with a Y stick, I am the life source."

"Please, I'm thirsty!" he demanded.

It reminded her of all the other days she had spent with mortals, being cornered into conversations like this, and it never did any good to tell the truth because they couldn't hear it, they brushed it off as soon as they could and kept on walking if you tried that. She remembered the last conversation like this when one of them became lost in her lands and how she had gotten more upset than she wanted to while trying to explain things that she'd taken oaths not to vouchsafe with any mortal:

"You think you have done something by seeing wisteria from your car and then telling me about it, or taking a grainy picture of it. I have not only bathed in, like you do only in your wildest fantasies for some reason, instead of doing something with your life...but I have been, I HAVE BEEN wisteria herself."

Nobody liked to hear these things, all mortals do is lie and want lies from you, "toned down" lies from you, as they put it. If you give them anything less than lies delivered apathetically, then they all mock you and raise their eyebrows to each other and say "she's INTENSE" in a horrifyingly knowing way that would make any person with even semi functional instincts want to bolt into a dead run.

Then sometimes some mortal who thinks they are wise will say to the girl, "Oh I understand. I was the same way, I had too many beautiful experiences, and it ruined the rest of life for me. That's the problem." All while trying to laugh about it.

This made the girl hate the mortals quite worse than anything else. They know about a mirage where they think they see water where there is none, but they do not contemplate that an opposite of the mirage also exists which is water being right there for you when you refuse to see it. They never factor in that the terms they coin based on the patterns they notice have equal reversals as patterns will. For example, fairies have more tales about the humans than humans have about the fairies.

"That is not the problem! THAT IS THE SOLUTION! No, no, no, no! I'd like to argue 'No' to that though, because I say that this is the SOLUTION" she could not contain the outburst.

You see why this Naiad girl could not make friends with the mortals? It is said some try but this naiad cannot. This one gets violently sick when she has to pretend, and yet the reason most mortals dislike her is that they say she pretends too often, such is their inherent blindness. She had to leave the man in need of water then. It wasn't cruelty, though as she would have gladly given him a drink if he had the capacity to sip.

plight of the representative

what have I done with my life?
Moved in and out of myself like a song
and in the large room of me you can hear it
loudly.

When you step outside where the moon shines
over the foxgloves-
The song sounds different from out there,
It has different things to offer
from a distance
that's why it's good to move out of yourself
when you can
to see from afar

that you never wasted a second.

I'm who you wanted to grow up to be,
except you let them stop you
and you want to frame that as my fault?
Nobody ever considers that as horribly
indelicate
treatment
to me!
all my bravery
all that leaping leaping leaping inside of me

which I splashed in valiantly
 is pushed off as luck

no one takes into account how beautiful
everything is, and that IS the problem:
living in that much denial
because they've been made to
and been made too
much
ashamed
to notice it from an early age

I realize they never tell you
when you buy a plant
how lovely every night of your life will be
when the vine grows up and into
an arbor you can rest under

when your baby grows into someone
with feelings as acute as your own

nobody prepares you for these things

have you ever heard of a representative being
sent?
that's me
sent from the earth as the lawyer arguing on the
side of life herself
 to remind you

February California

my heart is fit to burst through bows and ribbons
and go singing into the wind like a winged
valentine who has been supplied with a voice
box
when I get into a car with Misty and Manny to
go ANYWHERE!
getting into the car with other people usually
makes me feel hesitant, ready to bolt, but with
Misty and Manny we are in our office, our art
studio and our secret meeting place, a mobile
garden shed flying through clouds up and down
the very real, old purple mountain we live on.
my soul hasn't been set to automatic rejoice
mode like this in a long time and
if I'm capable of feeling free and whole in a car
with someone or two someone's when it never
happened before, this raises entire communities
and municipalities of questions inside of me:
 what else am I capable of enjoying entirely that
I'm sure I hate?
something less than jolted, but sort of tilted me
awake:
this was the thing,
not painful, not a crash, not a blister:
fun

where I'd never found fun to exist before
I could be someone else
and it might not even hurt

Nights Breathe

On the way to the bison bone marrow market
I saw one streetlamp still on at 10:21 am in the
long row of romantic old streetlights
I thought with a lurch: am I her? Do I try too
hard? Is what I'm recognizing here mySELF?
Do I work myself to death at times when it
makes zero difference anyway
i.e. when the sun is shining?
Some of us just can't turn our bulbs off so easily.

This girl kept talking and talking and talking and
when I could finally get a word in I said:
"Yes but-yes but-yes BUT ISN'T who you ARE
more than what happens to you? Isn't who you
are more than what goes on externally? Or the
circumstances you react to? Isn't who you are
buried and protected somewhere else and doing
something else than what others around you do
to you or what you observe? And isn't it kind of
your job to find out about that? To go scouting
for it?"
        I stood there after trying to hear her
refutation, but she froze and couldn't tell me
anymore. My fault, I'm sure. Do I try too hard?
Is that who I'm recognizing here? Myself?

Was I the girl trying to tell me these things, but I
wouldn't listen? Amorphous -
Is she the streetlight that won't be put out
 which is called brave when someone else does
it, but wasteful when I do?
some kind of moral ataxia
impaired coordination
or an allergy to taking responsibility
which they call a worthy character trait

When in despair I remember how even if it's
daytime now
we all know nights breathe,
all of us have felt and heard a night's breath, it
isn't just pretty words.
Some things the mortals can be laid back about,
you see?
They won't ever fight you when you mention
that a night breathes and
this puzzled me at first, it seems like a concept
far above them
given the caliber of other things they will argue
with you about
still
the mortals can surprise you. I think I forgot to
mention this, but they can !
Recuperative,
incipient
and they have their moments.
Some of us can't just turn our bulbs off so easily.

ACKNOWLEDGEMENT

Thank you to my mom for never once censoring my reading which would have DESTROYED my life.Thank you to everyone who has bought me notebooks throughout my life, especially my mom and dad and Z. Maston B. Thank you to my dad Breck for reading a doll sized Walden to me and my dolls as a toddler, SKNAHT to Landon and more than anyone to Viola Whimsy for spending every Christmas Eve watching boisterous singing rats drink red wine the way God intended. Thank you to Corah the tiger cub and Delmar Sensi Uqualla, Delmer and Anita Uqualla, Misty and Manny, Nan Ronnie Brown and Storm. Thank you to my maternal cousins for whom all my stories get jumpstarted on the haybales: Isabel, Octavia, Elias, Azalea, Gwen, Addie and Brayden, Jade and Eve. Thank you to Aunt Karen Holt for videotaping the Charlotte Waters collection, Reise, Ryder, Rory and Remi and special thank you to my Aunt Maggie who used to transcribe my stories for me after my tiny hands would get worn out from writing for so long when I was a kid. Thank you to Ambrose, Gunther and Madison and of course the inspirational writer Miss Iris Kai. Thank you to my treasured travel companions Aunt Alice and Uncle Brian, Uncle Jonathan for many things but especially for sharing his mom with me, and EVERYONE knows I am my Aunt Heather's girl. Thank you to Aunt Shorty a character for the ages. Thank you to all my Grandparents for buying me so many books: Pauly Grandparents, Barnhart Grandparents and Binkley Grandparents and particularly to my Pop for telling me the mouse stories and Nana Pam for writing coneflower stories with me as a kid. Thank you to JJLW, WBPW, Brynn and Bristol Lee Primrose: she of the endless mid morning wagon ride singalong. Thank you to Aunt Krista and the three who were in the room with me when I wrote most of this: Baby Cinnamon, Turner and his twin Peach Pie Jones. Lastly yet vitally thank you to Justice Govain, Tyler Feld, Elektra and Eros.